Pebble® Plus

Let's Take a FIELD TRIP

A ZOO FIELD TRIP

by Isabel Martin

Consulting editor:
Gail Saunders-Smith, PhD

Content Consultant:
R. Michael Roberts, DPhil
Curators' Professor of
Animal Science
University of Missouri

CAPSTONE PRESS
a capstone imprint

Pebble Plus is published by Capstone Press,
1710 Roe Crest Drive, North Mankato, Minnesota 56003
www.capstonepub.com

Library of Congress Cataloging-in-Publication Data
Martin, Isabel, 1977– author.
 A zoo field trip / by Isabel Martin.
    pages cm. — (Pebble plus. Let's take a field trip)
Summary: "Simple text and full-color photographs take readers on a virtual field
trip to the zoo"— Provided by publisher.
  Audience: Ages 4–8.
  Audience: K to grade 3.
  Includes bibliographical references and index.
  ISBN 978-1-4914-2098-0 (library binding) — ISBN 978-1-4914-2316-5 (pbk.) —
ISBN 978-1-4914-2339-4 (ebook PDF)
  1. Zoos—Juvenile literature. 2. Zoo animals—Juvenile literature. I. Title.

QL76.M37 2015
590.73—dc23   2014032322

Editorial Credits
Nikki Bruno Clapper, editor; Juliette Peters, designer;
Gina Kammer, media researcher; Tori Abraham, production specialist

Photo Credits
Dreamstime: Anankkml (top), cover, Rebekah Flory (right), 17, iStockphotos: ansaj
(left), 13, IS_ImageSource (middle left), 19, kali9, (middle right), 5, 7, kgrahamjourneys,
15, THEPALMER, 11; Newscom: Photoshot, 21; Shutterstock: angellodeco, cover,
GUIDENOP, cover, Iryna Dobrovynska, cover, 1, littleny, 2, 22, My Life Graphic, 3,
Sailorr, 9, Sean Pavone, cover, Tratong, cover

Note to Parents and Teachers

The Let's Take a Field Trip set supports national curriculum standards for social studies
related to institutions, communities, and civic practices. This book describes and illustrates
a class field trip to a zoo. The images support early readers in understanding the text.
The repetition of words and phrases helps early readers learn new words. This book also
introduces early readers to subject-specific vocabulary words, which are defined in the
Glossary section. Early readers may need assistance to read some words and to use the Table of
Contents, Glossary, Read More, Internet Sites, Critical Thinking Using the Common Core, and
Index sections of the book.

Printed in the United States of America in Stevens Point, Wisconsin.
092014   008479WZS15

TABLE OF CONTENTS

A SPECIAL SCHOOL DAY

Today is field trip day.

Your class is going to

the zoo!

AN ANIMAL TOUR

Giraffes live in big pens. Their long tongues help them grab leaves. Some zoos let visitors feed the giraffes.

Tigers are popular
zoo animals. You can
see them rest or walk
back and forth.

See the jellyfish

swim in their tanks.

Jellyfish pump water

in and out of their

bodies to move.

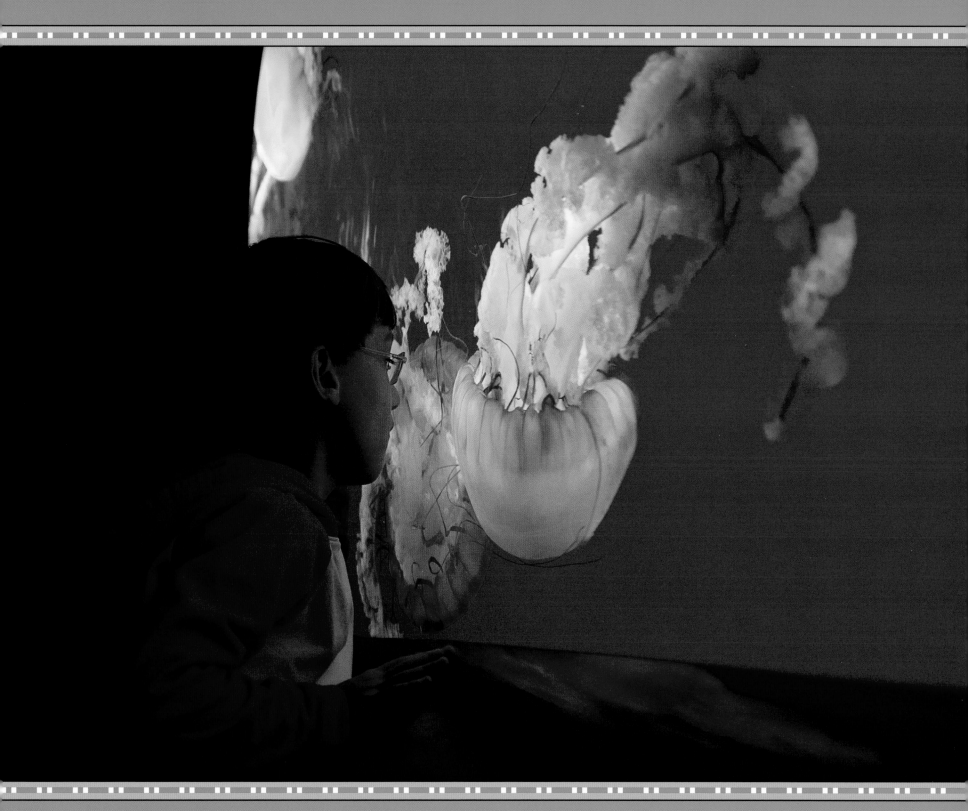

FUN AT THE ZOO

Some zoos let visitors touch certain animals. Visitors can pet and feed sheep, goats, and horses.

Zoos have special events every day. You can watch birds of prey at a bird show.

ZOO WORKERS

Zookeepers work with the animals. Zookeepers feed animals and keep their spaces clean.

Zookeepers also teach
visitors about zoo animals.
They hold snakes and
other animals for visitors
to touch.

Zoo veterinarians keep zoo animals healthy. Visitors sometimes get to watch vets work. You can learn a lot on a field trip to the zoo.

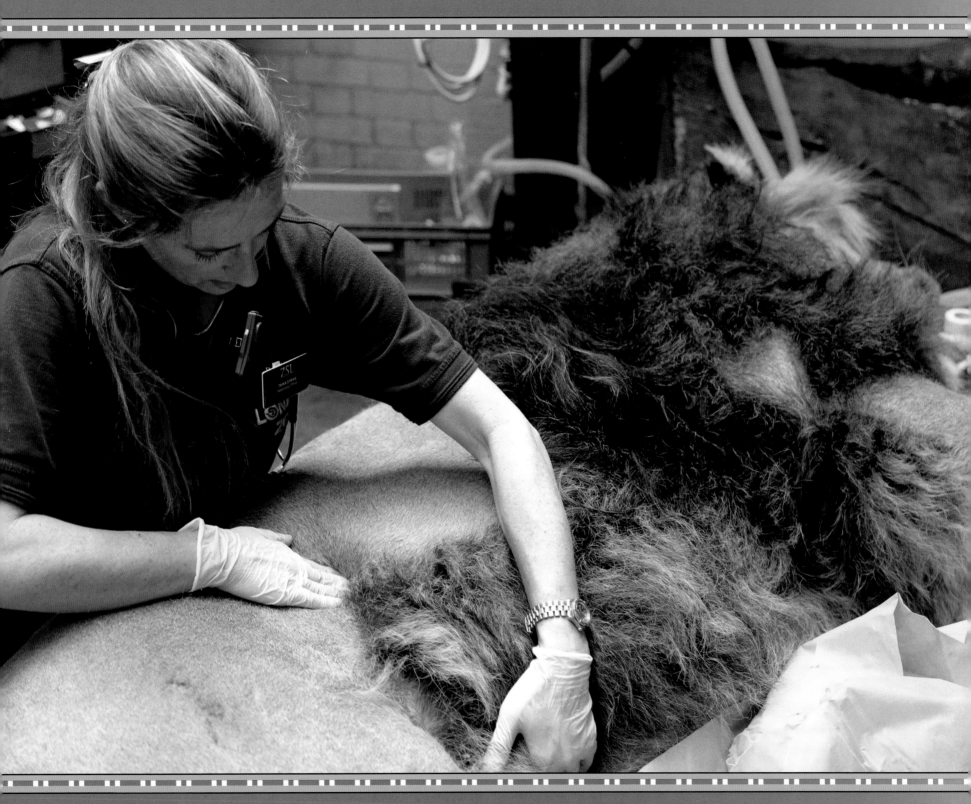

GLOSSARY

bird of prey—a meat-eating bird such as a hawk or an eagle

field trip—a class visit for learning something new at a place outside school

jellyfish—a sea animal with a soft, almost clear body and tentacles; a jellyfish is shaped like an umbrella

pump—to empty or fill using a pushing and pulling motion

tank—a glass cage where a sea animal, lizard, or amphibian lives

veterinarian—a doctor who treats sick or injured animals; veterinarians also help animals stay healthy

zookeeper—a person who takes care of the daily needs of animals in a zoo

READ MORE

Bleiman, Andrew. *ZooBorns!: Zoo Babies from Around the World.* New York: Beach Lane Books, 2010.

Curtis, Jennifer Keats. *Animal Helpers: Zoos.* Mount Pleasant, S.C.: Sylvan Dell Publishing, 2013.

Krull, Kathleen. *What's New? The Zoo! A Zippy History of Zoos.* New York: Arthur A. Levin Books, 2014.

INTERNET SITES

FactHound offers a safe, fun way to find Internet sites related to this book. All of the sites on FactHound have been researched by our staff.

Here's all you do:

Visit *www.facthound.com*

Type in this code: 9781491420980

CRITICAL THINKING USING THE COMMON CORE

1. What are three activities that visitors can do at a zoo? (Key Ideas and Details)

2. Look at the pictures. What does a zookeeper do to take care of animals? (Integration of Knowledge and Ideas)

INDEX

Word Count: 150
Grade: 1
Early-Intervention Level: 15